Senior Living

Senior Housing
Senior Retirement
The Best Places For Seniors To Retire
To Cheaply, How To Find The Right
Housing And Strategies For Living
Comfortably

By Ace McCloud
Copyright © 2013

Disclaimer

The information provided in this book is designed to provide helpful information on the subjects discussed. This book is not meant to be used, nor should it be used, to diagnose or treat any medical condition. For diagnosis or treatment of any medical problem, consult your own physician. The publisher and author are not responsible for any specific health or allergy needs that may require medical supervision and are not liable for any damages or negative consequences from any treatment, action, application or preparation, to any person reading or following the information in this book. Any references included are provided for informational purposes only. Readers should be aware that any websites or links listed in this book may change.

Table of Contents

DEDICATED TO THOSE WHO ARE PLAYING THE GAME OF LIFE TO **WIN**

KEEP ON PUSHING AND NEVER GIVE UP!

Ace McCloud

Be sure to check out my website for all my Books and Audio books.

Introduction

I want to thank you and congratulate you for buying the book, "Senior Living, Senior Housing, and Senior Retirement: The Best Places For Seniors To Retire, How To Find The Right Housing For Retired Seniors, Good Living For Seniors, And The Best Strategies For Seniors To Live Comfortably."

This book contains proven steps and strategies on how our beloved senior generation can get the most out of their retirement, from suggestions on what types of housing to select and where to settle down, to what to do with all that free time that their careers had previously taken up.

If you are nearly retired (or have already made the jump), or have a loved one that is nearing retirement age, this book will help ease any worries you or they may have regarding the tough decisions that lie ahead. Rest assured, going through retirement should be an enjoyable, painless transition from one phase of your life to the next. This book is intended to assist you in making your golden years as good as they can be.

Chapter 1: Congratulations On A Well-Deserved Retirement . . . Now What?

You made it! Congratulations on a major life accomplishment. You have worked extremely hard your entire life, saved your money, and have finally reached the point where you can stop working, kick your feet up, and relax . . . or so you thought.

While most people think of retirement as a time of stress-free and endless happiness filled with work-free days, long golf outings, and laughter-filled lunches with friends, being retired also requires some very serious decisions to be made.

You have earned every minute of your retirement, as you have spent the last couple of decades (the better part of your life, in fact), working to support not only yourself but your loved ones as well, not to mention your fellow citizens through your tax contributions. It's now time for them to support you, and give someone else a chance to work as hard as you did.

Given that approximately 10,000 baby boomers retire every day, the important decisions made by retirees and their families will be contemplated throughout households across America. The most pressing questions once you decide to stop working are, "Where will you live?" "In what type of housing?" and "What will you do with all of your free time?"

These questions are not meant to cause you discomfort, but rather to aid you in realizing that to spend your retirement years happily, it's important to plan ahead as soon as possible regarding issues of housing, health, and how to stay active.

Chapter 2: The Best Places To Retire To

While most people may find it ideal to stay put in their home after retirement, it may not be financially possible to do so, even if receiving monthly payments through Social Security, pensions, or private retirement accounts.

This being the case, it's never too early to consider where you might want to move to once you've reached retirement age. While the thought of leaving your long-time home may be stressing, just know that there are places around the country (and increasingly the world) that are geared specifically towards helping people like you adjust to that enormous retirement move.

Top Retirement Cities In The United States

Albuquerque, NM
Home to the University of New Mexico, Kirtland Air Force base, and national research laboratories, Albuquerque also attracts retirees with its very low cost of living, yet very high quality of life. Low housing prices keep the median monthly housing payment for those age 60 and above at $1,150 with a mortgage, $358 for those who own a home without a mortgage, and $657 for those renting.

For those seniors who no longer can drive or want to live car-free, the city provides for plenty of low-cost, safe, and healthy ways to get around. For just 35 cents, seniors over the age of 62 can take advantage of the busing system. And for the exercise-minded, Albuquerque boasts over 400 miles of paths and trails for bikers.

If you can stand the high temperatures (over 90 degrees F in summer) and high elevation (meaning thinner air and more fatigue during physical activity), then this beautiful city just might be for you.

Pittsburgh, PA

If you are a professional and collegiate sports fan, then this east coast city is the place for you. Pittsburgh is home to the world-famous Pittsburgh Steelers of the National Football League, and also home to the National Hockey League's Pittsburgh Penguins and Major League Baseball's Pittsburgh Pirates. You can also catch Division I football and basketball action at the University of Pittsburgh, and even though Carnegie Mellon University is more famous for its world-class technology programs, its Division III teams can still offer affordable and exciting entertainment.

The retiree who values high quality medical care above all else need look no further than this Pennsylvania city, which is home to the UPMC-University of Pittsburgh Medical Center, one of the top university hospitals in the nation. Not only is the center ranked nationally in 14 adult specialties, it ranks 10th nationwide in geriatrics.

And getting around to all of those sporting events, as well as the variety of museums, the ballet, symphony, and zoo that Pittsburgh features should not be a cause for concern. Citizens age 65 and over, with proper ID, can ride for free on the bus, the T (light rail and subway system), and the distinctive Mon Incline, Pittsburgh's antique cable cars.

With all of these great features, it comes as a surprise that the median monthly price paid by renters age 60 and older is only $590. Those with mortgages shelled out $1,079 per month, and those without mortgages get by with just $435 per month for housing.

While not nearly as cheap (or as warm and sunny) as many other southern and southwestern cities, if staying near family on the east coast is a priority, then this former steel town is worth a look.

St. Louis, MO

Though the distinctive feature of St. Louis may be the famed Gateway Arch, it is the other free attractions that make this a top destination for retirees. The zoo, science center, and a great mix of art and other museums, along with the 111 parks covering 3,250 acres offer seniors plenty of things to do at no extra cost.

Like Pittsburgh, this Midwestern city is a sports fan's delight, being the home of the Rams (NFL), Cardinals (MLB), and Blues (NHL). Plus, the area has plenty of college sports teams to follow, most notably the Division I University of St. Louis Billikens.

Also in town is the highly acclaimed teaching hospital Barnes-Jewish Hospital/Washington University, which garnered 14th place nationwide in geriatrics and national rankings in 15 other specialties.

In terms of housing, retirees still paying off their mortgage are looking at a median payment of $1,186 per month, while those who have paid it off already are spending only $442. Renters can expect to spend about $657 per month in rent.

If you can overlook the rising crime rate, then St. Louis, which also offers a solid bus and light rail system, could be your Midwestern retirement destination.

Columbia, SC

If southern comforts are your cup of tea, then you may want to look into South Carolina's state capital, Columbia. Offering the best of both big-city life and easy southern living, this metro area combines a very low cost of living with numerous recreational activities.

Retirees interested in pursuing higher education during their golden years can take advantage of the free tuition available to state residents over 60 (provided they are not working full-time). Performing arts enthusiasts will also find enjoyment from the Columbia Museum of Art, South Carolina State Museum, two ballets, philharmonic orchestra, and several theater groups. Finally, diehard golfers will marvel at the dozens of beautiful golf courses in or near Columbia.

And to get around town to all of those great events, residents age 60 and older pay only 75 cents to ride the bus.

Homeowners with a mortgage age 60 and older pay a median of $1,107 per month, while seniors with no mortgage pay only $350 per month. And renters of the same age group spend about $712 per month.

Throw in warm weather year-round, and it's not hard to see why this small (yet at the same time large) southern city with cheap housing and lots to do comes in near the top of the best retirement destinations in the US.

San Antonio, TX

If Tex-Mex culture is more to your liking, then San Antonio, a beautiful Texas metropolis with plenty of Spanish flavor left over from its not-too-distant past, may be your stop.

For seniors looking to earn some extra income on the side and keep busy, San Antonio's tourism industry offers plenty of employment opportunities. There are more than 20 million tourists per year that come to play the more than 50 golf courses, walk the 68 miles of park trails, experience Sea World, have fun at Six Flags Fiesta Texas theme park, and enjoy the many Tex-Mex music and food festivals held throughout the year. And, of course, let's not forget the Alamo.

Retired veterans may also find comfort in the large military presence in and around the city, as San Antonio is home to Fort Sam Houston, Randolph Air Force Base, Lackland Air Force Base, and Brooks City-Base.

As with the other top retirement spots, traveling around town to all of the many sites is extremely convenient and cheap, as San Antonio offers reduced fares to seniors age 62 and over. Between the many bus routes and three VIA streetcars (which operate 7 days per week), all historical and recreational points of interest are easily accessible without the need of a personal motor vehicle.

As far as housing goes, senior citizens age 60 and older can expect to spend about $1,155 for a home (monthly median with a mortgage), or only $398 for a home without one, while renters spend about $660 per month.

Best of all, warm and sunny San Antonio sits in the great state of Texas, which has no state income tax, making this an ideal place to stretch your retirement money.

If none of the above cities seem appealing to you, here are the top 25 cities in the USA to retire to according to the December 2012 edition of Money magazine: starting from number one and ending at number twenty five, some more cities for you to look at are: Albuquerque, New Mexico – Portland, Oregon – Louisville, Kentucky – Tucson, Arizona – Austin, Texas – Winston-Salem, North Carolina – St. George, Utah – Traverse city, Missouri – Coeur d'Alene, Idaho – Saint Augustine, Florida – Kalispell, Montana – Sevierville, Tennessee – Fredericksburg, Texas – Bellingham, Washington – Bloomington, Indiana – Huntsville, Alabama – Lynchburg, Virginia – Iowa city, Iowa – Athens, Georgia – Danville, Kentucky – Fort Payne, Alabama – Prescott, Arizona – Aberdeen, South Dakota – Summerville, South Carolina – Ottawa, Kansas.

Top Retirement Cities Abroad

For many, retirement is an opportunity to travel and see new places that they were unable to visit during their working lives. That's why foreign retirement locations are becoming ever more popular among American seniors, who are not only looking to see the world, but are also looking to take advantage of some very favorable exchange rates abroad which will greatly increase their purchasing power.

Keep in mind, however, that a huge downside to retiring abroad is that you will see your family and friends much less frequently than if you stayed close to home (or elsewhere in the states). But if holiday visits once or twice a year are enough, and you value experiencing new cultures (with a healthy dose of adventure), then here are five great retirement destinations outside of the United States.

Medellin, Colombia

Given that this Latin American nation spent the last couple of decades earning a reputation for drug-related crime, it might surprise you to learn that it has become a great retirement destination abroad. Much has changed since the Colombian army killed famed drug lord Pablo Escobar and brought cartel violence under control.

Lately, Medellin has been experiencing a sort of rebirth, with its architectural renaissance and blossoming tourist industry. Though year-round, spring-like temperatures permit daily walking, the very modern public transportation system (which includes a metro and tram) connects all of the city's neighborhoods, and the many parks, libraries, and museums contained in them.

For those concerned about making sure they can get back to the states from time to time (and not inconvenience visitors too much), Jóse María Córdova

International Airport is only 19 miles to the southeast, and offers nonstop flights to Florida cities Miami and Fort Lauderdale.

Additionally, Medellin is home to five of the top hospitals in Latin America, which is why it has become a popular destination for medical tourism. Though Medicare does not cover overseas medical care, the very favorable exchange rate makes paying out of pocket for services a workable option.

While not as cheap as other Latin American destinations, $1,500 a month would be more than enough for a retired American couple to live on. So if you can overcome feelings of worry that the last 20 years or so of seeing cartel crime on the news has brought, then Colombia's second-largest city might have your name on it.

Bilbao, Spain

If you feel more comfortable in a European city, then the heart of the Spanish Basque country may be for you. Perfectly situated in the northern part of the country near the French border and the Pyrenees Mountains, you can expect mild temperatures year round, and can easily access the beautiful Spanish coastline with a quick drive.

Getting back to the states will also not be a problem, as international Bilbao Airport is located a short 7 miles away (about a 15 minute cab ride) and features flights to the US.

Bilbao's state-of-the-art hospitals and clinics are top notch, and conveniently, the city also features many 24-hour pharmacies, a definite plus in a country known more for its midday siestas than customer service.

On the downside, Spain is much more expensive than retirement venues in up-and-coming nations. An American couple will most likely need about $3,500 a month to get by comfortably. However, you will not need a big budget to entertain yourself, as there are plenty of cheap activities for you to enjoy. Hop on the low-cost public transportation system (which includes rail and bus), and visit the world-famous Guggenheim Museum, stroll through the miles of parks, or head to the beach, which is less than an hour away.

Perhaps the biggest draw for seniors who value culinary delights is the region's world-renowned cuisine. The Basques have always been known for having some of the world's top dishes, and Bilbao and the surrounding area will not disappoint.

George Town, Malaysia

If you are looking for a destination well off the beaten path, consider hot and humid George Town, Malaysia.

Already known to foreigners in need of affordable yet reliable medical services, George Town has been slowly nurturing its medical tourism business for years. There are plenty of hospitals and clinics in and around this exotic Malaysian city.

The biggest drawback may be the distance from home, as reaching the states will require at least one connecting flight, and at least a full day's travel. However, Penang International Airport is a close 11 miles to the south, and can be easily accessed from the city center.

Malaysia in general is very friendly towards retirees, as is evident by the program called Malaysia My Second Home. Successful applicants can look forward to perks such as long-term residency status and discounts on major purchases and car imports. Even without the special program, George Town is still very affordable, as an American couple can live extremely well for about $1,500 a month.

While the city may not be as modern as others, you will quickly become enamored with this former British colonial city as you spend hours on end walking the ancient, historic streets sampling authentic Malaysian food from street vendors and appreciating the beautiful architecture. And instead of always using the bus, be sure to hop on the city's trishaws every once in awhile, as these cycle-powered cabs have become one of George Town's most entertaining and distinctive features.

And don't worry about being able to communicate. Due to its past ties to the British Empire, English is still very widely spoken.

Dubrovnik, Croatia

If you want to be in Europe without paying European prices, then consider the "Pearl of the Adriatic," as Dubrovnik is known. You won't get a typical tropical climate, as temperatures range from the mid 40's in winter to the mid 80's in summer. But what you will get is more history than you can take in.

A small city with Old World charm nestled between the beautiful countryside of Croatia and the sea, Dubrovnik provides seniors looking for a healthy mix of history, architecture, and culture with all of the above. Among the most historic sites are the 14th-century monastery and the medieval wall surrounding the city.

To take a break from sightseeing, retirees can head to the beach, but be sure not to miss the many cultural events such as the Dubrovnik Film Festival, Opera Festival, and yes, even Fashion Week.

For your health needs, you can visit General Hospital Dubrovnik, located conveniently in the center. And while bus service is available, you may want to try walking as much as possible so that you don't miss out on all of the undiscovered corners of the city.

Like George Town, Malaysia, Dubrovnik is a bit of a trek from the states. The airport is located about 10 miles from the city center, and from there, you'll most likely change flights once or twice (in some major European city) to get back home.

And while this historic city by the sea is one of the more expensive in Croatia, it's still much more affordable than other more popular Mediterranean locales, allowing an American couple to live very comfortably with just $2,700 per month.

Tlaxcala, Mexico

Situated amid the lovely mountains of Mexico, the mild-weathered city of Tlaxcala is located about an hour from major metro areas Puebla (1 hours) and Mexico City (2 hours), where seniors can go for international nonstop flights to the US, and also for high-quality care at major hospitals (though Tlaxcala does offer smaller treatment facilities).

With its brightly colored colonial-era buildings, Tlaxcala has managed to maintain its historical charm, and the wandering retiree will find traces everywhere of its Spanish past. Offering a much slower pace of life than the two bustling cities around it, and a significantly lower crime rate (since it has thus far avoided the violence brought on elsewhere by Mexico's drug war), visitors can take in such attractions as the Plaza de la Constitución, which features plenty of beautiful trees, fountains, archways, and colorful murals depicting the state's history.

The views are also not too shabby, as it sits near Malintzin, one of the tallest volcanoes in Mexico. And though it attracts plenty of tourists, prices remain appealing, as an American couple can get by modestly with only $1,500 per month.

And while the city is too small to support a large public transit system, you'll quickly find that walking the stone-lined, ancient streets are not worth missing, as is the enormous poncho market which takes place on weekends.

If none of these cities appeal to you, here is a list of 21 very popular cities to retire to from around the world as listed in the June 2012 edition of Money magazine. These cities are: Abruzzo, Italy - Ambergris Caye, Belize - Boquet, Panama - Cayo, Belize - Cebu, Philippines - Chiang Mai, Thailand - Copper Coast, Ireland - Costa de Oro, Uruguay - Cuenca, Ecuador - Georgetown, Malaysia - Granada, Nicaragua - Hoi An, Vietnam - Hua Hin, Thailand - Istria, Croatia - Kuala

Lumpur, Malaysia - Languedoc, France - La Serena, Chile - Medellin, Colombia - Mendoza, Argentina - Panama City Beaches, Panama

If you enjoy Spain, then the cities of Malaga or Cadiz located in the South of Spain in the province of Andalucia may be right up your alley. The weather is great and it is much cheaper to live here than in the North of Spain. English is almost a second language here and is a favorite retiring spot for many British seniors.

Another favorite spot to retire for many is the Canary Islands, a Spanish archipelago located just off the northwest coast of mainland Africa. Some of the favorite islands are Tenerife and Gran Canaria. The weather is warm all year long, with access to the ocean and beautiful beaches. It is also very cheap to live here, about one thousand dollars a month to live comfortably.

Chapter 3: The Best Housing For Seniors

Along with deciding where you'd like to live, soon-to-be retirees also need to consider what type of housing will best suit their needs going forward. It's important to keep in mind that not all of the housing options discussed below may be available in all locations worldwide. But here are some ideas on what type of residence would suit your retirement goals.

Staying Put

The easiest option is to simply stay in your current home, which can be a great idea mainly because you would still be around the friends and family you spent years getting to know in your current neighborhood, and would not feel the social isolation that many people feel when they move to a new place. As long as the maintenance work required isn't overwhelming (i.e. grass cutting, roof repairs, snow shoveling, etc.), aging at home is something to consider. Just be sure to look into support services in your area, to prepare for the time when you will need some assistance performing daily functions both in and out of the home.

However, there can be some drawbacks of staying in the same place. If you had children, you probably picked your current home partially because of the quality of the schools, which tends to drive local property taxes, over time, through the roof. Since you don't have school-age children anymore, it doesn't make sense to spend such a large amount of your fixed income supporting a school district that your family does not utilize anymore. Even with the tax reductions that are usually offered to seniors, you are probably paying a lot more for your current home than you would be if you downsized elsewhere.

Also, you have spent the better part of your life working hard and saving up for the day when you could focus on yourself. If moving to a warmer climate or a new country has been lifelong dreams of yours, you should not put them on hold any longer to appease those around you. You deserve to spend your retirement any way you please, and if moving elsewhere makes you happy, then do it.

Independent Living

Used to describe housing arrangements that have been designed with senior citizens in mind, independent living has come to include settings such as senior apartments, senior housing, retirement communities, and retirement homes. Structures of this nature can be condominiums, apartment complexes, and even detached homes. A distinctive feature of this type of housing is that the design was done with senior citizens in mind, incorporating things like easier navigation, more compactness, and assistance with property maintenance. More luxurious independent living sites offer recreational centers that can host dances, dinners, concerts, and game nights.

Assisted Living

The term 'assisted living' has come to encompass many names, as it may now be referred to as board and care, adult care home, residential care, congregate care, sheltered housing, adult group home, or alternative care facility. Unlike an independent living center, staff is usually available 24 hours a day, as seniors in this facility tend to need a bit more help with daily activities, such as taking medication.

Units come in all different styles, with some being individual apartments with scaled-down kitchens, to others that consist of just a private room. Most sites usually offer common areas for dining and social events, and depending on your budget, you may have to share a room with another retiree.

If you require a bit more attention than independent living, but don't quite yet need the round-the-clock care of a nursing home, then an assisted living facility may be for you.

Nursing Home

Outside of a hospital, a nursing home offers the highest level of care and attention that a senior can receive. While still providing the amenities of independent and assisted living facilities, such as the common dining areas, a nursing home also offers constant medical supervision, as they keep licensed physicians, registered nurses, and occupational and physical therapists on hand.

A nursing home is a great choice if you need some time to recover from a recent hospitalization, or have reached the point where your health is deteriorating and just cannot manage on your own.

Continuing Care Retirement Communities

Conveniently, senior citizens can find all three levels of care in one place with a Continuing Care Retirement Community (CCRC). After starting out under independent living care, you can move up to assisted living and then nursing home supervision as your changing health requires, without changing locations. Units are often purchased as you would a condo, with an adjustable monthly fee that will increase depending on the level of care you need.

The great thing about CCRC's is that if your spouse or close friends are housed in the same community, you don't have to be separated from them should your health worsen to the point where you would require greater medical attention.

Chapter 4: Living Good In Old Age

Now that you have your housing issues all squared away, the most pressing question is, "What will you do with all of your free time?"

Experts agree that one thing all retirees have to be mindful of is keeping active. The sudden shock of not going to work for most of the day can leave you feeling lonely and useless, so it's important to keep busy and dedicate yourself towards other pursuits, regardless of what they are. Here are some ideas for what you can do to pass your retirement years happily and productively.

Continue Working

While it may seem counterintuitive, many retirees decide to not leave the work force right away. Whether for financial reasons or simply because they genuinely enjoy working, it may be wise to consider continuing to work for a bit longer. It doesn't necessarily have to be in a full-time capacity either. Many employers would be happy to keep their most experienced employees around part-time so that they can mentor younger and middle-aged workers who have much less experience, and they often employ retirees as educators.

If you are the entrepreneurial-type, perhaps starting a small business is the move to make. Try to pick something with very low start-up costs that can eventually run itself over time once your team of assistants is in place, such as a website or a small clothing store. This way, you don't have to commit all of your free time to it, and should it not be successful, you will not have placed yourself in great financial risk.

Go Back To School

For the lifelong learners that have always had the idea of going back to school sitting in the back of their minds, the golden years are the perfect opportunity to do so. Many state universities offer free tuition to senior residents, giving them the perfect chance to keep their minds stimulated with discussions on ancient Rome, lab experiments, ceramics classes, and much more.

Learn A Language

Contrary to popular belief, it is never too late to learn to speak a new language. If you have always been enamored with a certain language and culture, then dedicate yourself to studying a little bit every day. Having the internet at your disposal brings all the languages of the world to your very living room, as you can access websites to help with your pronunciation, download texts from libraries across the globe, purchase textbooks and have them sent to your home, and even find language partners to practice with (both online and in your area to meet with face to face). Spending 30 minutes to an hour studying everyday, you will be having conversations in a foreign language in no time.

Travel

Retirement is the perfect time to see those near and far off places that you have always dreamed of visiting. Whether you want to take in some historic sites, some breathtaking views, or sample some exotic cuisine, use your retirement years to see all of the places you weren't able to go to while you were working. And don't limit yourself to a short visit. Consider spending a month or two in a certain place before leaving, in order to get to know some of the locals well and really immerse yourself in the local culture, maybe even picking up a solid foreign language foundation to build off of when you return home.

Traveling is also a great way to meet new friends in your area. Look online for some travel groups that plan trips regularly, and think about doing a weekend with them to see if you connect with the group.

Your local travel agencies also plan group trips with seniors in mind. And there are always traditional cruises you can go on geared towards seniors, so you won't be bothered by crying babies or partying 20-year-olds.

Volunteer

Even if volunteering has never been your thing, consider giving it another try during retirement. It's a healthy and inexpensive way to get out of the house and enjoy yourself, meet new people, and give back to your community.

If you feel confident tutoring a certain school subject, local schools and afterschool programs would be happy to have you, as would the children who would surely appreciate some extra individual attention.

To still feel connected to your previous profession, you could mentor college students planning to enter into your field of practice, such as medicine, or help out at a local clinic during blood drives. And if you don't find an organization that is offering volunteering opportunities that interest you, then start one. There isn't a neighborhood in America that doesn't have problems that need to be addressed, and often times, a little dedication and goodwill from some volunteers is all that is required to solve many problems.

Find A Hobby

Your post-work years are the perfect time to take up a hobby, or continue on with an existing one. Whether you play an instrument, hammer away in a woodshop, or knit winter hats for friends and family, find something that really motivates you and will keep you both mentally and physically active.

And don't limit yourself to spending time on your hobby alone. Hobbies are a great way to meet other like-minded individuals, so look into joining or starting a group, performing or presenting your items at craft fairs, and attending conferences and trade shows.

Exercise

Last but not least, make sure to stay physically active during retirement by getting plenty of exercise. Keeping active will be great for your health in the long run, both physically and mentally.

As you get older, your body will naturally wear down, but there are still many great workout activities that retirees can participate in well into old age. You can play tennis, golf, bike, hike, walk, and swim to name a few.

Try to stay away from things that will put enormous amounts of stress on your body, and instead engage in activities that will get you outside, not put strain on your body, and allow for social interaction. Light weightlifting has been found to have tremendous benefits for men and women late into their lives. For some great strategies to stay healthy into your later years, be sure to check out my book: Anti-Aging Cure.

Chapter 5: Strategies for Living Comfortably

When you retire, of course, you want to make yourself as comfortable as possible. There are many ways to do this, and by this age, I am sure you know quite a few things that work well for you. Here are some other ideas if you haven't thought of them already.

Besides having a husband or wife, a pet can be one of the most comforting things in life. Dogs are great companions and can definitely help keep you motivated to get outdoors more and go on walks. If you're looking for a pet with less maintenance, then cats are ideal. There is nothing nicer than sitting in your favorite chair with a cute kitty curled up in your lap, purring.

It is also a good idea to have a steady routine that you do every day. Many of the most successful people in the world have planned out what routines work best for them, and they do them religiously every day. Some good things to include in your daily routine is exercise, some sort of social interaction, be it by telephone, e-mail, or just meeting face-to-face with friends. Make a list of all your favorite activities and things that you like to do, and then try and incorporate as many as you can into your daily routine. It's also a good idea to have your diet planned out as well. Eating correctly is a great way to stay energetic and healthy.

Another thing that will bring you tremendous peace of mind is having all your finances in order. Make sure you are doing your research on all of your expenditures. Sometimes all it takes to save some money is a few phone calls that are dedicated to finding a better deal. With your finances in order, you will know exactly how much money you have to spend each month on enjoyable things and activities. These can range from nice dinners, to massages, to traveling, hobbies, and more. Good shoes and a comfortable wardrobe are also a good investment. You will find things run much smoother when you have a plan and you know exactly how much money you have to spend.

Lastly, you want to make your home or living area is as comfortable as possible. Being organized is a great way to make sure you have everything you want, where you want it. If you're not good at organizing, you can hire someone to help you with it relatively inexpensively. Make sure your most important items and things that you use most often are easily accessible. It's also a good idea to decorate your living area with some of your favorite pictures that you've collected over the years. Furniture that you enjoy is also very important. It may be worth spending that little bit of extra money to get that top-of-the-line recliner or sofa that you always wanted. A good bed is also a priority. Air beds have been found to be excellent for relieving back pain that normal mattresses can cause. If you live in a colder climate, a good space heater would be a good investment. Taking the time to fix up your living area just the way you want it will make you more comfortable and happier as well.

Here are a few ways to make your home more enjoyable and safe. Install handles and grip bars in the bathroom to assist in getting in and out of the shower/bathtub. Also, be sure to use rubberized bath mats inside and outside of the bathtub to help prevent an accident. It is a good idea to use a night light in areas near the bathroom for when you need to get up in the middle of the night. Room darkening window treatments are also good for sensitive eyes and can promote longer more restful sleep. A good electric can opener is always nice to have and a telephone with a larger keypad can make dialing phone numbers much easier. Also, it is a good idea to have important numbers installed in the speed dial of a phone that can be easily accessed with a single push of the button. When you move into your new place take your time and set it up the way you want. Once everything is organized and set up for your enjoyment, the only thing left to do is enjoy your retirement.

Conclusion

I hope this book was able to help you learn what to expect when you reach retirement age (if you are not there already), and how to deal with the decisions that lie ahead.

The next step is to talk with your loved ones about where you'd like to live and in what type of housing, so that the best possible decision can be reached. Also, start to plan what activities you think might interest you, so that you can hit the ground running. Remember, it's never too late to do anything in life.

Above all else, don't look at retirement as coming to the end, but rather as a new beginning.

Finally, if you discovered at least one thing that has helped you or that you think would be beneficial to someone else, be sure to take a few seconds to easily post a quick positive review. As an author, your positive feedback is desperately needed. Your highly valuable five star reviews are like a river of golden joy flowing through a sunny forest of mighty trees and beautiful flowers! *To do your good deed in making the world a better place by helping others with your valuable insight, just leave a nice review.*

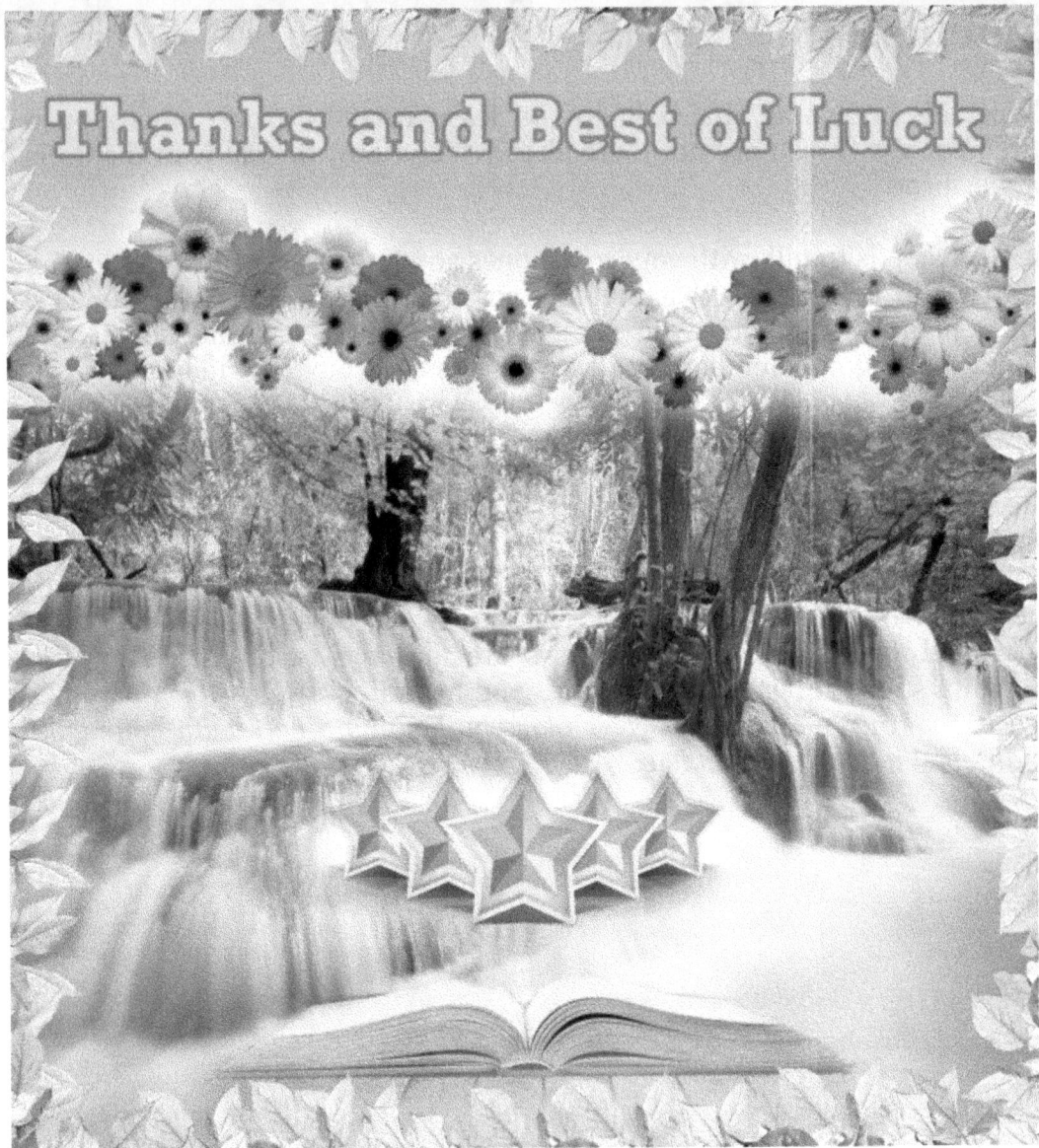

Thanks and Best of Luck

My Other Books and Audio Books
www.AcesEbooks.com

Health Books

ULTIMATE HEALTH SECRETS

HEALTH

Strategies For Dieting, Eating Healthy, Exercising,
Losing Weight, The Mediterranean Diet,
Strength Training, And All About Vitamins,
Minerals, And Supplements

Ace McCloud

ENERGY
ULTIMATE ENERGY

Discover How To Increase
Your Energy Levels
Using The Best All Natural
Foods, Supplements
And Strategies For A Life
Full Of Abundant Energy

Ace McCloud

RECIPE BOOK

The Best Food Recipes
That Are Delicious, Healthy,
Great For Energy And Easy To Make

Ace McCloud

MASSAGE THERAPY

TRIGGER POINT THERAPY
ACUPRESSURE THERAPY
Learn The Best Techniques For
Optimum Pain Relief And Relaxation

Ace McCloud

LOSE WEIGHT

**THE TOP 100 BEST WAYS
TO LOSE WEIGHT QUICKLY AND HEALTHILY**

Ace McCloud

FATIGUE
OVERCOME CHRONIC FATIGUE

Discover How To Energize
Your Body & Mind So
That You Can Bring
The Energy & Passion
Back Into Your Life

Ace McCloud

Peak Performance Books

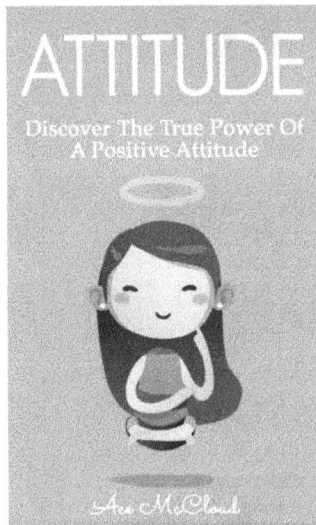

SUCCESS
SUCCESS STRATEGIES
THE TOP 100 BEST WAYS TO BE SUCCESSFUL
A c e   M c C l o u d

Ace McCloud
HABIT
The Top 100 Best Habits
How To Make A Positive Habit Permanent
And How To Break Bad Habits

MOTIVATION
MASTER THE POWER OF MOTIVATION
TO PROPEL YOURSELF TO SUCCESS
Ace McCloud

ATTITUDE
Discover The True Power Of
A Positive Attitude
Ace McCloud

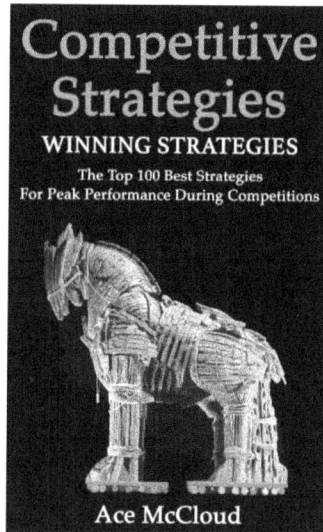

Be sure to check out my audio books as well!

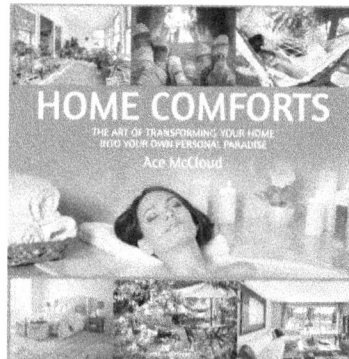

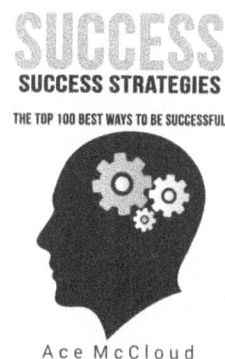

Check out my website at: **www.AcesEbooks.com** for a complete list of all of my books and high quality audio books. I enjoy bringing you the best knowledge in the world and wish you the best in using this information to make your journey through life better and more enjoyable! **Best of luck to you!**

www.ingramcontent.com/pod-product-compliance
Lightning Source LLC
Chambersburg PA
CBHW080633030426
42336CB00018B/3184